BEIJING
THE CITY AT A GLAN(

Sanlitun
Revel in trashy Beijing nightlife
late-night eating and Chinese p
for attention around the Worke
See Neighbourhoods

Art Zones
The avant-garde have colonised defunct
factories and farming villages. Enclaves
include Dashanzi (see p012), East End Art
(p034) and Song Zhuang (p100).

Forbidden City
The last emperor moved out in 1924, leaving
9,999 rooms in mothballs. The major halls are
undergoing repairs ahead of the Olympics.
See p010

CCTV HQ
This twisted frame of yin by Rem Koolhaas
and Ole Scheeren, due to open in 2008, offsets
the yang of business district skyscrapers.
*East 3rd Ring Road, between Guanghua and
Jingguang Bridges*

Wangfujing
No longer just street food and scam artists.
Tread Zhou Enlai's favourite dance floor at
the rebranded Raffles Hotel (see p017) and
have drinks at the Beijing Grand (T 8518 1234).
See Neighbourhoods

Mao Mausoleum
The Chairman had asked to be cremated,
but thanks to his hangers-on, his enbalmed
corpse lies in state in a crystal coffin.
Tiananmen Square

Old Legation Quarter
Style envoy Handel Lee is jazzing up the
former American Embassy as an upscale
dining, arts and entertainment venue.

INTRODUCTION
THE CHANGING FACE OF THE URBAN SCENE

Only a year or two ago, Beijing did not really merit a Wallpaper* City Guide: modern design-wise, there lacked a critical mass of class. Why, it was asked, have double-digit GDP growth and the investment of tens of billions of dollars in the 'best Olympics ever' not delivered such perks as a Michelin-rated Peking duck eaterie? Or a five-star courtyard b&b? Or a neo-traditional, state-sponsored schema of architecture that one could call a success?

Well, consider the stresses on the city and its people. For the past two decades, it's been the urban laboratory of a nation trapped in transition, between free markets and protectionist monopolies, nationalism and globalisation, central planning and corruption, and, most woefully, between deprivation and decadence. And does anyone really know where the country is heading today? '*Chai-na*' (pronounced 'China') is a Chinglish pun currently in vogue here. It means 'demolish that'. Fittingly so, for the capital Beijing has vaporised much of its past in order to materialise its future.

But there's something addictive about the place, as any *laowai* (foreigner) who has caught the 'Beijing bug' will tell you. While the city boggles the mind with its contradictions, it remains a hotpot of possibilities. It must be this mix of tensions that intoxicates its inhabitants – who only seem to do things the hard way – and makes them struggle on. And in the past few years, their struggles have borne some smart new venues. Smart enough for our pages.

ESSENTIAL INFO
FACTS, FIGURES AND USEFUL ADDRESSES

TOURIST OFFICE
Dongcheng Tourist Info Centre
10 Dengshikau Xilu
T 6512 3034

TRANSPORT
Car hire
Avis
T 8406 3343
Beijing Top A Car Service
T 6438 1634
Taxis
Beijing Taxi Company
T 6831 2288
Tourism Taxi
T 6515 8604

EMERGENCY SERVICES
Ambulance
T 120
Emergencies
T 110
Fire
T 119
Police
T 110
24-hour pharmacy
Beijing International SOS Clinic
BITC Jing Yi Building
5 Sanlitun Xiwujie
T 6462 9100
www.internationalsos.com

EMBASSIES
British Embassy
11 Guanghua Lu Jianguomenwai Beijing
T 5192 4000
www.uk.cn
US Embassy
3 Xiu Shui Bei Jie
T 6532 3831
beijing.usembassy-china.org.cn

MONEY
American Express
28 Jianguomenwai Street
T 6515 7671
travel.americanexpress.com

POSTAL SERVICES
Post Office
Jianguomenwai Dajie
East 2nd Ring Road
T 6512 8114
Shipping
UPS
1 Jianguomenwai Dajie
T 6505 5005
www.ups.com

BOOKS
Oracle Bones: A Journey Between China's Past and Present by Peter Hessle (Harper Collins)
Remaking Beijing: Tiananmen Square and the Creation of a Political Space by Wu Hung (University of Chicago Press)

WEBSITES
Art/Design
www.artrealization.com
Newspapers
www.chinadaily.com.cn

COST OF LIVING
Taxi from BCI Airport to city centre
€13.40
Cappuccino
€3.40
Packet of cigarettes
€1.70
Daily newspaper
€1
Bottle of champagne
€65

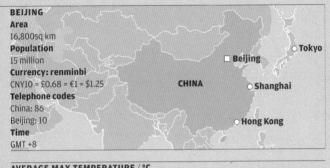

BEIJING
Area
16,800sq km
Population
15 million
Currency: renminbi
CNY10 = £0.68 = €1 = $1.25
Telephone codes
China: 86
Beijing: 10
Time
GMT +8

Tokyo

Beijing

CHINA

Shanghai

Hong Kong

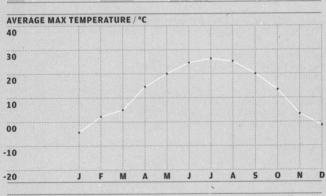

AVERAGE MAX TEMPERATURE / °C

| 40 |
| 30 |
| 20 |
| 10 |
| 00 |
| -10 |
| -20 | J F M A M J J A S O N D |

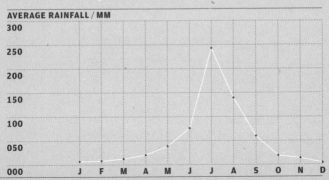

AVERAGE RAINFALL / MM

| 300 |
| 250 |
| 200 |
| 150 |
| 100 |
| 050 |
| 000 | J F M A M J J A S O N D |

NEIGHBOURHOODS

THE AREAS YOU NEED TO KNOW AND WHY

To help you navigate the city, we've chosen the most interesting districts (see the map inside the back cover) and underlined featured venues in colour, according to their location (see below); those venues that are outside these areas are not coloured.

GOLD COAST

The build-up on East 3rd Ring Road yields a mountain range of largely anonymous glass and steel skyscrapers. Soon, though, Rem Koolhaas' remarkable new HQ for the state broadcaster CCTV will redraw the landscape. Ghettos of quietude can be found in the old embassy area, except the on the Russian streets of Yabao Lu. Ritan Park is the best-manicured public space north of the Yangtze. Climb the rockery for a great vista of Chaoyang business district.

UNIVERSITIES

Liang Sicheng, the founder of China's seminal School of Architecture at Tsinghua University, begged Mao to save the walls of the Old City and build a new one to its north-west. Alas, he declined. But the new digital economy is making up for Mao's miscue. The area is losing its image of punks and poor scholars to computer cities, artsy internet cafés and towers of tech geeks. Only peasant software pirates keep it real.

WANGFUJING

A hopscotch through the twin poles of modern Chinese history. The doors of the Forbidden City (see p010) open daily, while those of adjacent Communist Party enclave Zhongnanhai are ever closed. Bordering the Great Hall of the People, a big classical box, is a futuristic bubble – Paul Andreu's National Grand Theatre (see p014). Though mostly a shopping arcade for the masses, Wangfujing is slowly getting trendier.

EAST SIDE

Between the airport and the city lie a few former farmers' communes and migrant shanty towns, and many more art villages, international schools, driving ranges, villas and luxury apartments. Borrowed names range from Palm Springs to Park Place to Yosemite. With all the bric-a-brac, spas and cafés around the Holiday Inn Lido and the bustle of arts zones like Dashanzi, aka 798 (see p012), suburbanites practically never need venture downtown.

OLD CITY

Once home to concubines, warlords and literati, the labyrinthine blocks surrounding the emperor's old hood are prime real estate once again. In the interim, they were ravaged by Maoist collectivisation and pre-Olympic modernisation. Only height limits on new builds and serious gentrification have helped salvage what remains. Nanluogu Xiang leads the lanes going Bobo (bourgeois bohemian).

SANLITUN

The untameable Hydra of Beijing nightlife. Expats christened the leafy embassy zone with a few pubs in the early 1990s, and beloved hang-outs were soon born on Sanlitun Nanlu. Now, huge swathes have been flattened and new complexes are moving in. Between the Workers' Stadium and the Workers' Gymnasium, the former Gongti 100 Bowling and Tennis Center is a mecca of clubs and local cuisine.

LANDMARKS

THE SHAPE OF THE CITY SKYLINE

Credit the Mongols, who under Kublai Khan established the Yuan dynasty (1271-1368), for hatching Beijing's master plan. It called for the Dadu (Great Capital) to be laid out along a symmetrical grid, with a central axis bisecting the Imperial Palace. Even today, this renders Beijing's layout – as architecturally incomprehensible as it seems – self-explanatory. The city is its own compass.

The early Ming emperors erected the Forbidden City at the core, placing temples in four directions, to the Sun, Moon, Earth and Heaven. The Qing dynasty Manchus kept that basic schema intact. Not the case for Mao's planners, who mowed down the city wall to build the 2nd Ring Road, many of whose bridges lie where the city gates once stood. This set the pattern of concentric ring roads that have rippled outwards ever since. Outside the ancient city, campus and cadre life has long been concentrated on the west side, with diplomatic and now corporate life to the east. There Beijing finally has a downtown of sorts, around the China World Trade Center.

If only getting around the grid was so simple. Beijing's huge kilometre-square blocks make most neighbourhoods unwalkable, and while the subway is good for getting to the central sites, it's otherwise limited (a few new tentacles are due to open this year). As for the roads, they carry 1,000 new vehicles each day, including the Hyundai sedans that have replaced Beijing's little red taxis. *For full addresses, see Resources.*

Forbidden City

Chairman Mao 'faced south', just as any emperor of yore would, on declaring his dominion from the Gate of Heavenly Peace in 1949. But superstition, it is said, stopped him from ever stepping foot inside the Forbidden City itself. The Son of Heaven's old digs really sparkle under a winter dusting of snow and are equally as impressive at night; stroll around the ghostly moat into the outer yard at the Wumen gate. The walls of the 'Purple Forbidden City', as it is alternately known, are 'pig's-liver red'. The bricks are of white lime and glutinous rice and there are egg whites in the cement.
North of Tiananmen Square,
www.dpm.org.cn

Dashanzi Art Zone

It was here that Beijing's avant-garde first stumbled on a post-industrial 'promised land', the proletarian slogans on the walls providing a powerfully gimmicky context. The area was soon dubbed 798, after the Bauhaus-style Factory 798 electronics plant at its core, now the 798 Space exhibition centre (above). Sections were mothballed by the late 1980s and pennies per square metre rents in the mid-1990s attracted the first resettlers: the Central Academy of Fine Arts (T 6477 1019). Art publisher Robert Bernell moved in and seminal artists, like Huang Rui, followed. Dark forces nearly spoiled it. Citing safety hazards, 798's owner wanted to put up high rises in its place, but well-connected denizens of the community saved the day. *4 Jiuxianqiao Lu, T 6437 6248, www.798space.com*

Bell Tower

Over beers on the terrace of the Drum 'n' Bell Bar (T 8403 3600), expat *hutong* dwellers often debate which of the time-keeping towers is aesthetically superior: the Drum (Gonglu) to the right or the Bell (Zhonglu) to the left. The Bell often takes the cake. It's a sympathy vote. Its gawkish, medieval form went up in the late 1300s, but was soon consumed by fire and not rebuilt until the 1700s. Meanwhile, the bell was removed because it tolled too softly. According to legend, such were the struggles of one foundry man to cast a bigger, louder bell, that his daughter threw herself into the molten bronze to stir the sympathies of the gods. She left behind one of her slippers, and on stormy nights the new bell was said to emit a spooky note sounding like the word *xie* (shoe). *Gulou Xidajie*

National Grand Theatre

When architect Paul Andreu won the 1998-99 competition to fill the 'big pit' beside the Great Hall of the People, critics lampooned his bubble of glass and titanium as everything from a duck egg to a dung pile. But defenders saw an iota of Chineseness in its circle-in-square geometry. It's perhaps too early to say if Andreu's laid an egg or not.
West side of Tiananmen Square

HOTELS
WHERE TO STAY AND WHICH ROOMS TO BOOK

More than five years after Beijing snatched the 2008 Summer Olympic bid, a shortlist of the city's finest hotels looks much the same as it did before. But that's set to change, with city apparatchiks promising 800 star-grade hotels with 130,000 rooms by 2008.

One of two new Ritz-Carltons opened in autumn 2006. Set on 'Financial Street' (1 Jinchengfandong, T 6601 6666), on the still not-so-happening west side, the outside is a clean sheath of glass by Skidmore, Owings & Merrill; inside, Hirsch Bedner & Associates has forged a *wabi-sabi* futurism distinct from its previous work in hotels like the St Regis (see p018). While this opening is aimed at the banker set, the more fashionably located Ritz-Carlton Central Place, by Wimberly Allison Tong & Goo, will serve the corporate jet-setter in the east, when it finally opens east of Chang'an Dajie. Marriott is adding a 591-room monster on the same plot and a Four Seasons is under construction too, as are two Hyatts. At the Park Hyatt, located on top of the 63-storey Beijing Yintai Centre (2 Jianguomenwai Dajie), American architect John Portman's design for the upper floors resembles a Chinese lantern.

There's also a buzz about boutique properties, but less action, though Bulgari is reportedly in the market. For now, you'll likely be out at the Commune by the Great Wall (see p097). No matter where you stay, count on paying for it as the Olympics near.
For full addresses and room rates, see Resources.

Raffles Beijing Hotel

After austere updates in the 1950s, 70s and 90s, this hotel reopened as part of the Raffles group in June 2006. The original 1900s façade, blending French and oriental influences, has been preserved, along with the arches, the inlaid stone in the lobby and the parquet floor in the lounge, where Zhou Enlai is said to have entertained North Vietnam's Ho Chi Minh. Fashion prince Benny Ong has clad the bellhops in cream ascots and interior designer Grace Soh has dressed up the rooms. Only the veneer of the floors and furniture leaves the place feeling a bit too new. Stay in four-poster elegance in the Landmark Suite (above), savour modern French cuisine at JAAN and sip a Singapore Sling in the Writers Bar. *33 Dongchang'an Jie, T 6526 3388, www.beijing.raffles.com*

St Regis Hotel
Even within the embassy district, the
St Regis smacks of a colonial oasis.
The Roman-style pool gives the gym
a spa-like quality, while the Club Wing
Lobby (pictured) and Garden Lounge,
all palm trees and Versailles mirrors,
have inspired many a chintzy imitator
among China's nouveau riche developers.
21 Jianguomenwai Dajie, T 6460 6688,
www.stregis.com/beijing

Red Capital Residence

This jocularly named hospitality brand is the brainchild of US China hand Lawrence Brahm. He started with the Red Capital Club (T 8401 6152), a home-style supper club, and recently opened a retreat, the Red Capital Ranch (see p092). All three are receptacles for his collection of curios from the corridors of Communist Party power, as seen in the Capital Residence's reception room (above). If nostalgia means more to you than creature comforts, this centuries-old courtyard hotel is worth one sleepover at least. The Red Capital Residence has five rooms, which are dedicated to concubines, writers – Mao's embedded Long March biographer Edgar Snow and the doctor-cum-novelist Han Suyin – and, of course, to the Chairman himself.
9 Dongsi Liutiao, T 8403 5308,
www.redcapitalclub.com.cn

Lu Song Yuan Hotel

This 56-room hotel is set in the former residence of a fabled Qing dynasty Grand General. Sinophiles seeking out the 'real China' swoon over its mix of modern conveniences and musty authenticity. It comforts them with the feeling that Beijing isn't nearly the struggle it once was, yet it hasn't been completely lost either. That said, you should choose your room carefully. The hotel has one suite (above), with its own courtyard, but this lacks the cosiness and the mesmerising views of the corded clay-tile rooftops to be found in rooms on the second floor. It's an increasingly popular booking, so secure your reservation well in advance.
22 Banchang Hutong, T 6404 0436, www.the-silk-road.com

The Kerry Centre Hotel

Progressive and placeless, the Kerry exudes an aura evocative of the fact that it opened in 1999, the year China clinched its entry into the World Trade Organisation. Part of the Shangri-La chain, owned by Malaysian billionaire Robert Kuok, it's located along the Fortune 500 beltway and has become a hub for the brat pack of IT entrepreneurs. The décor in all the rooms, including the Deluxe (above), is contemporary-lite, with the Chinese characters for Kerry sewn on the pillows. The gym, with basketball and tennis courts, is the biggest of any hotel in town. The Kerry Mall offers good dim sum, but the big draw is the Centro Bar & Lounge (right). Originally a banal hotel lounge, it's now a jet-setter's haven, with sultry servers, music and fruity martinis crafted by award-winning bartender Bruce Li.
1 Guanghua Lu, T 6561 8833,
www.shangri-la.com

The Peninsula Beijing

The dank lobby and lavatory-tiled façade do date this hotel near the Forbidden City (see p010), but much has changed since it opened in 1989 as the Palace. In 2001, the worn gaudiness was damped down in favour of a few local touches, like silk Chinese screens, and a new sleekness, as seen in the 28 Beijing Suites (above). And in July 2006, the hotel was renamed The Peninsula. Surrounding Wangfujing has been transformed too. This may mean fewer *hutong* to meander down but more upscale restaurants to check out, in addition to the hotel's own super-chic eateries, Jing (overleaf) and Huang Ting, which offers some of the daintiest dim sum in town. What hasn't changed here is the global shopping, from Tiffany to Vuitton. That makes the lobby (right) a fun place to spy on whoever's buying.
8 Jinyu Hutong, T 8516 2888,
www.beijing.peninsula.com

China World Hotel

During the 1990s, the vermilion and gold foyer (left) of this Shangri-La venue was the city's power lobby. Others have come along since, but after a 2003 makeover it retained an incomparable sense of drama. Set within the China World Trade Center, the hotel is a favourite of both dignitaries and captains of industry. The downstairs shopping mall features a few idiosyncratic boutiques, while upstairs updated rooms, such as the Beijing Suite (above), are dotted with contemporary Asian art. The remodelled dining room is much brighter than most. The hotel and Tower 1 were constructed during the late 1980s, and with their subtle curves, the brown glass edifices are far more palatable than many that have since popped up.
1 Jianguomenwai Dajie, T 6505 2266, www.shangri-la.com

Shangri-La Hotel

Venture out to the west side of Beijing
and, despite its less cosmopolitan look,
there's a sense that this is where the real
movers and shakers operate. And some
of them – policy advisers, state bankers,
technology and property barons, and,
of course, celebrities – splash out here.
While this is another hotel that has aged
on the outside, it has kept its interior
fresh. Standard rooms are as commodious
as they come, and those facing east
overlook the Purple Bamboo Park. The
tea service in the lobby lounge (right)
is vintage Shangri-La, while the Cloud
Nine Bar, like its Shanghai counterpart,
is the nightspot to be seen at in the area.
The Garden Terrace, with its koi carp
ponds, has long been the scene of torch-
lit BBQs and Moon Festival celebrations.
Well, if it's good enough for Bill Gates...
29 Zizhuyuan Lu, T 6841 2211,
www.shangri-la.com

24 HOURS

SEE THE BEST OF THE CITY IN JUST ONE DAY

Beijing is a historic capital where the sites are all too often drably explained. It's an avant-garde city where cutting-edge art can be hard to find, and it's politically conscious, though your guide may leave you with the impression that the masses still dare not talk politics (fyi: they do). Too often, visitors go home content to rave about all the capitalism and construction. But there are ways to get further beneath Beijing's skin.

Grab a free English entertainment guide, such as *That's Beijing* or *City Weekend*. The best place to edify yourself is The Bookworm (Building 4, Nansanlitun Lu, T 6586 9507). Then scour the city by bicycle; ask your concierge how and where you can rent one – don't spend over 50 yuan on the rental, wear a helmet and lock up or prepare to forfeit your deposit. Head to any of the universities to find an 'English corner', where students meet up and try to hone their accents. Or check out how *les autres* of Beijing get on. Muslims congregate at Niujie Libai Si Mosque (88 Niu Jie, T 6353 2564) and Uighurs by the sites of what were once buzzing enclaves, at joints like Xinjiang Islam Restaurant (Xinjiang Provincial Government Office, 7 Sanlitun Lu, T 6833 5599).

Or take in Sunday mass at a state church. At the Jesuit-built Dongtang (74 Wangfujing Dajie, T 6524 0634) and Nantang (181 Qianmen Xidajie), the pastors include engaging English speakers. *For full addresses, see Resources.*

10.00 Hutong tour

The *hutong*, Beijing's folk ecosystem of alleyways, are slowly going the way of the Parisian arcades: they're dying. Planners said that they were protecting some of the old neighbourhoods within the 2nd Ring Road when the Olympics spurred urban renewal efforts in 2001. But preservation is often code for prettification: relics are saved, ramshackle brick-built *pingfang* homes are gutted. Among the displaced residents, the gripe often concerns not conservation but compensation. Around Houhai, the *hutong* of the future are Bobo: boutiques, brick lanes and breakfast nooks. Stop for coffee and a bite at the Vineyard Café (T 6402 7691), near the Lama and Confucius Temples. The Qianmen environs are tumbling as we type. For an example of not-so-bad urban renewal, head for the area around the Pudu Temple.

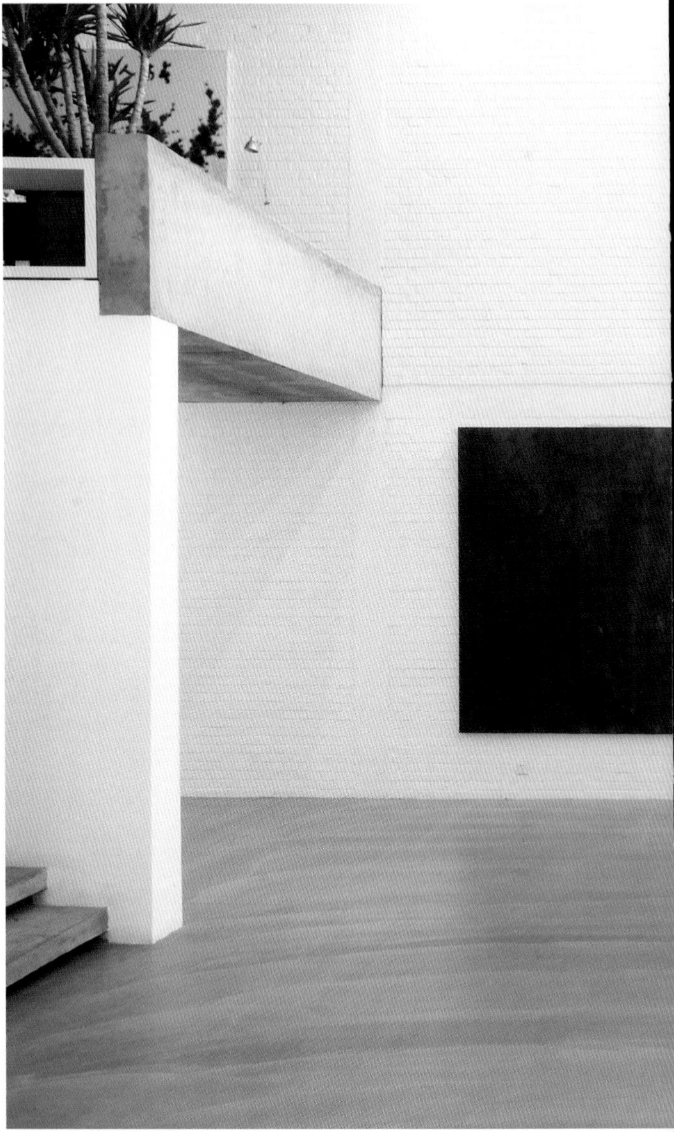

11.30 Gallery hopping
For a replay of the avant-garde's Big
Bang, start at the Dashanzi Art Zone
(see p012). Rising rents and busloads
of tourists are driving away many
artists there, so head for East End Art
(T 8096 5616), a zoned community
a few kilometres north in Caochangdi
village. Don't miss Ai Weiwei's most
recent space, the Galerie Urs Meile
(pictured, T 6433 3393).

14.00 Café Sambal

Cho Chong Gee, impresario of Malaysian cuisine, started out in this paint-peeled shoebox of courtyard chic, before opening the bar Bed (T 8400 1554) a block away. He and his wife are also planning two new places: a fresh and healthy Cantonese eatery nearby, with an open kitchen, to be called Paper, and Sambal Urban, a sequel to Café Sambal, which will be located in the Phoenix Town development. At Sambal, the free-spirited Gee still has a knack for making everyone feel like a regular. A chef from Kuala Lumpur rules in the kitchen. If you are tempted by the curry chilli crab or lobster with nyonya sauce, they must be ordered a day in advance. Watch out for Gee's mojitos – they're intoxicatingly good.
43 Doufuchi Hutong, T 6400 4875

18.00 Houhai

Seven centuries ago, the khans' engineers hooked up the ponds that we call Houhai (translated as 'Back Lakes') to the Grand Canal. By the Ming dynasty (1368-1664), the district was a fairground for élites, while in more recent decades, it took on a plebeian charm, as a hang-out for old men playing chess and virginal student couples. Today, Houhai is a pub crawl and a great place for a sunset drink. The trendsetter was No Name Bar (see p045), opened around 2000. Masses of lesser venues followed and, in mid-2006, officials pledged to close 60 to 70 of these around the banks. Nostalgia lovers should wander down Snuff Bag Alley (Yandai Xijie) or take in a threepenny opera at Gong Wang Fu or Prince Gong's Mansion (T 6616 8149).

21.00 My Humble House

For his pair of recently opened restaurants, My Humble House and House By The Park (T 6530 7770), Andrew Tjioe called on two Japanese design studios. My Humble House hits you right between the eyes at the entrance with a reflecting pool in front of the bar (above); just make sure you are not shunted off to the less airy side. The menu, which has Chinese and Continental choices, is curiously discordant for fusion cuisine, but the miso cod goes down silkily, and the shredded mango duck salad is a divine interplay of sweet and spicy. Teaser text on the menu bears the mark of JinR, the gastronomic diva behind the Green T House (see p046). So silverbait crisps are introduced thus: 'The heart speaks, I hear the pitter-patter, such captivating sounds.'
Beijing Oriental Plaza, 1 Dongchang'an Jie, T 8518 8811, www.tunglok.com

00.30 Rui Fu

For jaded China-pats, the opening night at Rui Fu was perhaps the high-society event of 2006. Valets waved their cars into the gates of a decaying fin-de-siècle manor, once the HQ of Republican-era strongman Duan Qirui. On this night, it recovered a tinge of its former splendour, courtesy of Henry Lee. The Tibet-loving Buddhist is the dark prince of Beijing clublife, his wife, Sally, the sorceress. Proprietor of Public Space, then Vogue, then Neo-Lounge, all now defunct, Lee wants Rui Fu to show how he and the city's nightlife are moving on up. Bathed in a Zinfandel glow, the space is somewhere between Tinseltown and colonial Shanghai: long, buttery white and country club-like, with private side chambers on the ground floor, a sunroom and a rooftop veranda.
3 Zhangzi Zhonglu, T 6404 2711

URBAN LIFE
CAFÉS, RESTAURANTS, BARS AND NIGHTCLUBS

Beijing is, officially, still in the first stages of socialism. Consequently, many hot spots look appropriately rough around the edges. Li Qun Roast Duck Restaurant (11 Beixiangfeng Hutong, T 6705 5578) is a famous dive. At Han Cang (13 Qianhai Dongyan, T 6404 2259), trust the bossy waitresses to order Hakka dishes for you. The view from the terrace at the Grand Hotel (35 Dongchang'an Jie, T 6513 7788) remains the best-kept secret in town. Brown's (Nansanlitun Lu/Gongti Beilu, T 6592 3692) does Beijing's best impression of a macho pub, while the city's metrosexuals prefer Centro Bar & Lounge (see p022). After sweeping Jakarta, Bangkok and Shanghai off their feet, art bar Face has a brand-new base (26 Dongcaoyuan, Gongti Nanlu, T 6551 6738).

Live music is a must in Beijing. YuGong YiShan (1a Gongti Beilu, T 6415 0687) showcases rockers on the ascendant, while cutting-edge bands perform at 2 Kolegas (21 Liangmaqiao Lu, T 8916 9197). The owner of D-22 (13 Chengfu Lu, T6265 3177) hosted Sonic Youth at his first joint in NYC and remains committed to the sounds of tomorrow. Hed Kandi Club (10 Dongsanhuan Beilu, T 6590 9999) has 'in' DJs but not the best location. Chinese jet-setters flock to mega-chains Babyface (6 Gongti Xilu, T 6551 9081) and Banana (22 Jianguomenwai Dajie, T 6528 3636). Desperadoes end up at Maggie's Bar (South Gate, Ritan Park, Guanghu Lu, T 8562 8142). *For full addresses, see Resources.*

Qu Na'r?

Designed by Ai Weiwei, and owned by him and some of his design-world cronies, this funky artists' dive is one of the newer, less fussed-over examples of a major culinary trend taking shape in China over the past five years: star artists turn restaurateurs, make minimalist spaces to hang friends' art and adapt the fresh flavours of distant provinces. Maybe it's not edgy enough, though: Qu Na'r? has been remodelled once already. It serves Jinhua-style Hangzhou cooking, and ingredients include salted meats, taro, lotus root and bamboo shoots. Order pork ribs with zong leaves, or any of the fragrant duck dishes. Among the stews, try the dry pot tea tree mushroom. Quiet and casual, this is a good place to wind down after a tough day of art villages.
16 Dongsanhuan Beilu, T 6508 1597

A21

Among a growing breed of artsy joints that modernise the pungent south-west flavours of Yunnan and Guizhou provinces, A21 is a dark horse. Owned by Taiwanese actor Gao Mingjun, it's slightly off the beaten path, but still draws the beautiful people into a capacious, unpretentious space. The interior is a little stark, but the beaded doorways to the washrooms and splashes of colour jazzily undercut the minimalism. And you can hardly go wrong with the menu. On the lighter side, the grilled fish with leeks is superb, as is the salad of wild greens. Those with heftier appetites should order the curried prawns, which distinguish themselves with piquant flair. The barbecued pork ribs arrive bulging on the rack, but the server will break them down for you, should you prefer.

21 Beitucheng Donglu, T 6489 5066

Dao

Submerged within a dark walkway off Houhai is the Guangfu Temple. During the Cultural Revolution, Red Guards pillaged the east hall. So this dining room (above) is the last remaining hall from a Daoist sanctuary built in the 1400s. Daoism was in vogue at the time, and Zu Yingying, an influential Ming dynasty eunuch, bought the land and built the temple. 'He thought that way his soul would be released from suffering,' the chef explains. In his tiny kitchen, precious little oil, MSG or hot spices are used. The *jin yu man tang* is a starch lover's dream: mashed potatoes with a yellow bean ragu, bordered by corn on the cob. Meals come *prix fixe* at CNY119 a head. Heated jars of 1980s vintage *huangjiu* (yellow wine) cost extra.
*Guangfu Temple, 37 Yandai Xiejie,
T 6404 2778*

No Name Bar

Ex-concert cellist Bai Feng is credited with triggering the re-gentrification of the 'Back Lakes' with this quaint, pot-planted, Hanoi-style café (above), which opened in 2000 unnamed (hence its name). Beer signs, neon and kitschy Lotus Lane have since overrun the shores. But Bai scored one back for the forces of good last year, opening No Name Restaurant (T 6618 6061) in the *hutong* across the bridge. The interior is a surreal mix, part New Mexico, part Ibiza, part Atlantis. Rooftop seating conjures up an image of a tiki island bar, except that the clay-tile roofs of an 800-year-old city surround you. The food is reworked from the sub-tropical flavours of tribal minorities in the deep south-west Yunnan province. The Dai-style lemongrass roasted fish is a treat.
3 Qianhai Dongyan, T 6401 8541

Green T House

From just a table or two in Beijing to trumpeted landings in Bangkok and New York, Green T House creator Zhang Jinjie found fame with starkly monumental design and earthy fusion food at eye-popping prices. Now she is simply known as Jin R, and some people visit just to see if all this posturing is really worth it. Funny, then, that she's currently one of China's foremost advocates of *wabi-sabi*, the Japanese aesthetic of unaffected beauty. Without the high-backed chairs, the Green T House (above and left) was nothing but a void. The newer venue, Green T House Living (T 136 0113 7132), located in the 'burbs to the east, is more of a mausoleum: white on white by day and gold on black at night.
Gongti 100 Complex, 6 Gongti Xilu, T 6552 8310, www.greenteahouse.com.cn

Garden of Delights

It was while Venezuelan architect Antonio Ochoa-Picccardo was working on the décor for RbL (see p054) that the owner told him he had an alleyway to unload. So emerged this awe-inspiring restaurant space. But for the skylights, it evokes an old subway tunnel. Dishes of fused South American flavours and killer desserts are served with a punch of abstract expressionism.
53 Dong'anmen Dajie, T 5138 5688

Le Quai
Part of a centuries-old mansion that
was transplanted from Anhui province,
the cinnabar-stained pillars, stairs and
carved lintels here form an arresting
site. Le Quai offers one of the inner city's
more scenic brunches, canalside on the
outdoor patio, and its dim sum makes
it a popular afternoon tea destination.
*East Gate, Workers' Stadium, Gongti
Beilu, T 6551 1636*

Pure Lotus

The theory of Buddhist purification Pure Lotus subscribes to is 'disenchantment through enchantment'. The monks behind this little fetishist experiment spare few details, whether on the cuisine or on the décor. The oversized menu is peppered with sutra-like nuggets of wisdom: 'Life: it's not one's body, but the nature of one's heart.' Alcohol is, of course, sacrilege here; instead there are energy tonics.

The wild Chinese yam drink can replenish a man's vitality, or a woman's hormone levels. Pure Lotus also specialises in the ancient art of replicating meat dishes with bean curd. Zen spicy stewed fish captures the flaky texture of the ever-popular *shuiyu*.
10 Nongzhanguan Nanlu, T 6592 3627

Zeta Bar

The flagship is in London's rejuvenated Hilton on Park Lane, and Zeta's looking to perform that same magic on the warped Hilton Beijing. The sprawling space, designed by Hong Kong firm Aedas, might as well be the foyer of a Bel-Air mansion. With any luck, Zeta will draw Chinese tabloid buffs who confuse the name with that of a certain Hollywood siren. Birdcages hold the drinks, while a mezzanine hosts the private parties and a glass 'show box' the VIPs. The bar stools glow. All of this, plus a glass spiral staircase, make Zeta considerably classier, though less private, than hotel rivals Centro Bar & Lounge (see p022) or Redmoon (see p061). The drinks are more straight-laced, and the sommelier is quite serious about the wine.
*1 Dong Fang, Dongsanhuan Beilu,
T 5865 5000, www1.hilton.com*

RBL

Down the block from his first art/dining
project, The CourtYard (T 6526 8883),
Handel Lee has imported an unabashedly
cosmopolitan concept: a restaurant/
bar/lounge. It's not been easy. The bar
and the restaurant were both overhauled
within a year. Now the chef is trying to
adapt Japanese fusion to 'local tastes'.
53 Dong'anmen Dajie, T 6522 1389,
www.rbl-china.com

Stone Boat Cafe

Editors at nightlife bible *That's Beijing* anointed Stone Boat 'Bar of the Year' in 2006. Few destinations are so peaceful, or reliant on Mother Nature. By day, Chinese literati take herbal tea and surf the wireless web, Russian traders pound afternoon beers and fishermen gather around the pond. At night, the boat becomes a secret party oasis within Ritan Park. Local bands drum up live jazz, folk and world beats on the bow. In winter, the scene turns positively Norman Rockwell, when children frolic on the frozen pond and the café serves up mulled wine and curative Chinese soups. Built in the early 1980s, this stone boat is a replica of the kind of structure that was once a fixture in the gardens of élites.
West Gate, Ritan Park , Ritan Lu,
T 6501 9986

Lan Club

Zhang Lan's restaurant chain South Beauty started out with a simple concept: sleek spaces for Beijing's bourgeois with clean-cooked Sichuan spice. Now Zhang and son Danny Wang are driving up the stakes in their latest venue, Lan Club, with a first for the capital, having lured Philippe Starck. With a whole floor of a mall in the LG twin towers to work with, Starck went berserk. There are Boffi chandeliers and a Starck classic: floating glass sheets holding vases and decanters. A mirrored, marble-inlaid sushi/oyster bar shimmers 1940s-style, and private rooms are wall-less, swathed instead in splash-painted canvas. Starck's space will infect fat cats and retrosexuals in different ways. And that's the beauty of it.

4th floor, LG Twin Tower, 12 Jianguomenwai Dajie, T 5109 6012, www.qiaojiangnan.com

Lan Club

Suzie Wong's

At the top of the stairs, a tangle of red faces and bronze legs on a Ming dynasty 'concubine bed' is the first clue: people here are hooking up. Like the movie from which its name and concept derive, Suzie Wong's was an overnight sensation when it opened in 2002. Most hipsters seem to be seduced by the chimera of a 1960s Hong Kong bordello, but that said, many a Western male has found his Suzie Wong here in 21st-century Beijing. The place has been recently remodelled and remains an after-hours institution. Bodies sprawl in the lounge, the dance floor pulses with Sino-techno, and the terrace is a fine place to chill and take calls.
1a Nongzhanguan Nanlu, T 6593 6049

Redmoon

With slatted wooden partitions, rust-hued lighting and dapper customers cavorting around a long, rectangular bar, Redmoon affects a slow-motion scene out of a Hong Kong noir flick. This is a lounge lovers' lounge, where dark corner seating allows patrons to huddle in private. The bar staff slice sushi and serve sake cocktails with sexy names. The only big question mark is whether the band appeals. Strumming power chords out of Chinese string instruments, the ensemble of leggy ladies in high-slit cheongsams rocks to such karaoke classics as 'Hotel California' and 'Sweet Child O' Mine'. Their earnestness makes it difficult to grin. Fortunately, there's plenty of space, should you wish to keep your distance.
Grand Hyatt Hotel, 1 Dongchang'an Dajie, T 8518 1234, www.beijing.grand.hyatt.com

INSIDER'S GUIDES

JENNIFER QIU, PR EXECUTIVE

Beijing is her home, but it took several years for Jennifer Qiu to learn to love it. As a student, she studied international trade and marketing in Zurich. Whenever she came back to visit, friends dragged her to the same old hang-outs, like Boys & Girls Club (68 Sanlitun Lu). After repatriating in 2003, Qiu had no job and Beijing was paralysed by SARS. But that's when she finally began to soak up the city. 'Now there are so many new places,' she says. 'I feel like, wow, I really love this town.'

Her favourite new perch is Rui Fu (see p039), where she counts owners Henry and Sally as pals. So is Handel Lee; his Icehouse, below RBL (see p054), is the place to hear the blues. To chill out, Stone Boat Cafe (see p056) gives her a 'sensation unlike any other place'. She finds all she needs for her coffee table at the Timezone 8 Editions bookstore (see p076) in Dashanzi Art Zone (see p012). Qiu describes herself as a 'very picky' eater, but she digs The CourtYard (95 Donghuamen Dajie, T 6526 8883). 'They brought modern fusion to Beijing,' she says. And to preserve her healthy glow, she opts for a treatment at the Dragonfly spa (60 Donghuamen Dajie, T 6527 9368). Like lots of true Beijingers, though, Qiu can never really go home again: the neighbourhood of her childhood is long gone. 'There are many things, like new roads, that Beijing needs,' she concedes, 'but all the destruction is very sad.'
For full addresses, see Resources.

ARCHITOUR

A GUIDE TO BEIJING'S ICONIC BUILDINGS

The schizophrenic history of China's last 100 years is refracted in its architecture. Beijing has served as a testing ground in the search for a modern Chinese stylistic identity, largely to its misfortune.

The drive for modernism began amid the civil warring that took place in the early 20th century. Stately buildings embraced neo-classical features, such as patterned struts and flying eaves, but only a few archetypes remain, including campus buildings at Peking University and the Peking Union Medical College Hospital (1 Shuaifuyuan). The next major period of creativity came during the 1950s, with the 10th anniversary of the People's Republic resulting in The Great Hall of The People (west of Tiananmen Square, T 6608 1188), Beijing Planetarium (138 Xizhimenwai Dajie, T 6825 2453), National Library of China (33 Zhongguancun Nandajie, T 8854 4114) and Workers' Stadium (Gongti Beilu, T 6501 6655). Then three decades of skeletal tenements followed.

By the late 1980s, the Communist Party had a new MO: 'market economy with socialist characteristics'. Postmodern structures with imperial roofs and ornamental pagodas soon appeared. More recently, to showcase Olympic China, officials looked to US-trained Chinese starchitects. Despite their quirky futurism breeding cuts and delays, excepting Steven Holl's Linked Hybrid residential omplex at Dongzhimen, the show goes on, as furiously as ever.
For full addresses, see Resources.

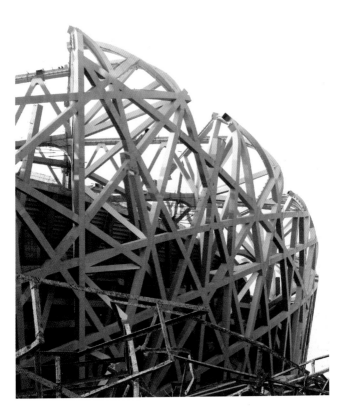

Olympic Stadium

Mongol conquerors placed their northern gate about here. Seven centuries on, Swiss-based Herzog & de Meuron landed the Olympic stadium bid with their 'bird's nest', partly thanks to input from Beijing art luminary Ai Weiwei. They soon became trapped in the convoluted politics of architecture in China. In 2004, a safety audit was held after a Paris airport terminal collapsed. Then upset about the un-Chineseness of the 'nest' and in a bid to halt gluttonous 'image projects', planners urged cuts. And so the 91,000-seat arena's retractable roof was shelved. But the official strategy failed somewhat, saving as it did only $36m (£19m) – less than 10 per cent of the total tab. Let's just hope the weather's dry come August 2008.
Olympic Green, T 6669 9185, www.en.beijing2008.com

National Swimming Centre
With the aim of being one of the most
spectacular venues of the 2008 Olympics,
Australian architects PTW and engineers
Arup have created a striking outer surface
nicknamed 'The Water Cube'. Inspired by
bubbles and organic cells, it will have five
pools — one with a wave machine — 17,000
seats and a solar energy-capturing roof.
Olympic Green, T 6669 9185,
www.en.beijing2008.com

Imperial Granary

Beijing's 'Xintiandi', they're calling it, after Shanghai's touristy arcade. But Xintiandi was minted from replicas of Old Shanghai *shikumen*, while half of this re-purposed complex consists of the old granaries of the Ming dynasty's emperors (the rest are faux). City planners wanted the agrarian look and pedestrian-friendly environs preserved, so they gave each unit only two parking spaces. Maybe that's why some weightier shops andrestaurants haven't moved in; the interiors of those who have don't impress. Still, yuppies will flock to Noble Family (T 5879 3179) and Rain Club (T 6409 6922), while the Xin Beijing Art Gallery bodes better for the future. For now, the Imperial Granary reminds us of how central Beijing could have remade itself more charmingly, but didn't.
22 Dongsi Shitiao

Dongbianmen Watchtower
In 2002, the city excavated the buried
Ming dynasty wall beside this tower,
bulldozing a block of ramshackle homes
and reclaiming thousands of original
bricks. The Ming Dynasty City Wall
Ruins Park (T 6527 0574) was duly built.
Illuminated after dark, it makes a pretty
nightscape. Also visit the Red Gate
Gallery (T 6525 1005) inside the tower.
Jianguomen Beidajie

SHOPPING

THE BEST RETAIL THERAPY AND WHAT TO BUY

Once upon a time, Beijing's only good tourist shopping was to be found at that mecca of mass-produced junk, the flea market, where migrant *getihu* (small entrepreneurs) gave you a run for your money. Alas, that changed when the infamous bazaar of ersatz brand names, Silk Alley, moved indoors (Xiushui Dongjie). But 'cheaper, cheaper' China lives on at Hongqiao (Tiantan Donglu, T 6713 3354), where the gems on offer include dyed freshwater pearls. There is also Panjiayuan Antique Market (Panjiayuan Lu, T 6775 2405), where the word 'antique' belongs in quotes. Upstairs you'll find posters of revolutionary agitprop and 1980s movies. For Asian urban gear at a discount, wander the Sanlitun malls Yashow, 3.3 and Nali.

More discerning shoppers will head to Qianmen, for Beijing's 'time-honoured brands' or *lao zihao*. For silk, visit Qianxiangyi (5 Zhubaoshi Jie, T 6301 6658) or Ruifuxiang (5 Dazhalan Xijie, T 6525 0764). For cotton slippers, head to Neiliansheng Shoe Shop (34 Dazhalan Jie, T 6301 4683) and for vitality pills, to Tongrentang Drugstore (24 Dazhalan Jie, T 6303 1155). Finding genuine antique furnishings is tougher. Peace Art Co (South Gate, Ritan Park, 17 Guanghua Lu, T 8562 2680) is one of the few downtown spaces with well-explained items dating from all the dynasties. Or, for an adventure, hire a car, drive east to the villages of Shibalidian and Gaobeidian and spend the day rambling from yard to yard.
For full addresses, see Resources.

Yin Shu

Beijing's pearl market might as well never have existed. Out at Dashanzi Art Zone (see p012), ensconced in the cross-hairs of art and commerce, Yin Shu is one of those East Side boutiques out to mine more ideas from a lot less. Shells, silver, crystal and semi-precious stones are combined to form hoops, chokers and other talismans. The shop's designer is a gallerist and sculptor from Sichuan, one of China's more romantically and artistically endowed provinces. Like most other jewellers in town, she has turned an obsessive hobby into a profession. Her creations nicely accent the couture of co-occupants EA West Fashion, a Guangzhou label that does sophisticated eveningwear in unassuming shades.
Zone A No 11, Dashanzi Art Zone, 2 Jiuxianqiao Lu, T 6437 3432

Spin Ceramics
Created by master ceramicists from
Hong Kong and Jingdezhen, China's most
legendary repository of porcelain, Spin's
work evokes an aesthetic derived from
nature; eggplant jars drip with red glaze,
and tea and sake sets bear the patina of
ground tofu. The only things less showy
than the pieces are the low prices.
6 Fangyuan Xilu, T 6437 8649,
www.spinceramics.com

SHOPPING

Timezone 8 Editions

Contemporary Chinese art found one of its earliest promoters in Texan Robert Bernell, who created the respected e-zine Chinese-art.com in the late 90s, then the publishing house Timezone 8 Art Books. Bernell's bookstore (left) found a natural home at the epicentre of the emerging scene – Beijing's 798. Housed in what was once the factory canteen, in an airy space designed by architects Mary-Ann Ray and Robert Mangurian, the shop sells an impressive list of titles on the Chinese visual arts, including Timezone 8's own English-language publications, which cover art, architecture, photography and design. The grass-roots art action may have shifted away from 798, but the Timezone 8 store still acts a hub, hosting artists' talks, book launches and film nights in English and Chinese.
4 Jiuxianqiao Lu, T 8456 0336, www.timezone8.com

Shanghai Tang

You can step into a Shanghai Tang store in New York, Paris or London, but there are a handful of items that you'll find only in the Chinese branches: three in Shanghai, four in Hong Kong, including the flagship shop in the Pedder Building, and the Beijing boutique (left) in the Grand Hyatt. The brand has recently collaborated with the Hong Kong-based Schoeni Art Gallery and a group of young Chinese artists to create a run of limited-edition 'Beyond the Canvas' products (on sale in Hong Kong). At the Beijing store, browse the range of homewares, including this bold bone china 'New Deco' tea jar (above), CNY1,220, patterned accessories and the trademark embroidered jackets, jacquard dresses and hand-knitted coats.

Shop 3-5, Grand Hyatt, 1 Dongchang'an Jie, T 8518 0898, www.shanghaitang.com

Liu Zaiping
There's a phantasmagoria of jigsaw-puzzle patterns and colours in the leather purses, wallets and decorative items on offer here. Clutch bags come with finger holes and angular cases will fit laptops. The designer's daughter filmed *Oxhide*, a movie about the family.
NB112, Basement 1, China World Shopping Mall, 1 Jianguomenwai Dajie, T 6505 8533

The Orchard

For many a downtowner, weekends in the suburbs tend to feature The Orchard. The brainchild of a West Virginian and her Chinese husband, this yarded country cottage is a surreal commentary on the divisions of the Beijing countryside. Expats flock here for the gourmet weekend buffet in the restaurant, which is better than those offered at some of the finest hotels. They digest brunch with a stroll in the marshy gardens, then stop at the shop. With the help of local villagers, The Orchard makes high-quality wooden tables, desks and humidors, wrought-iron candlesticks and homemade jams. It also stocks locally made soaps, jewellery, photographs, and sweaters and socks knitted by women from China's poor interior, who get a cut of the proceeds. *Sunhe Market, Jingshun Lu, Shunyi, T 6433 6270*

Plastered T-shirts

The proprietor himself admits: someone had to do it. *Hutong*-dwelling Londoner Dominic Johnson-Hill is aping the quotidian iconography of modern Beijing, both public and commercial, for hipsters and travellers. Plastered T-shirts fill that gaping hole for niche alternatives to the ubiquitous 2008 Games apparel. They thereby tap an irony that is somehow not shocking: while Beijing protects the international logo better than any other item in its history, a limey is pinching some of the city's classic motifs. Signage on the shirts comprises Goldfish soap, Yanjing beer, subway tickets and a stroke of the surreal – 1970s-style bikini beach resort decals for...Beijing. Most sell for the doubly lucky price of CNY88.
61 Nanluogu Xiang, T 134 8884 8855, www.plastered.com.cn

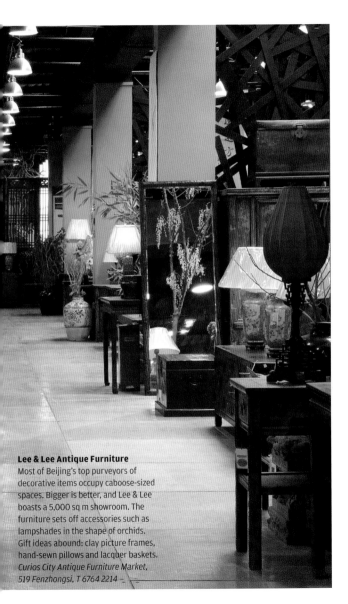

Lee & Lee Antique Furniture
Most of Beijing's top purveyors of
decorative items occupy caboose-sized
spaces. Bigger is better, and Lee & Lee
boasts a 5,000 sq m showroom. The
furniture sets off accessories such as
lampshades in the shape of orchids.
Gift ideas abound: clay picture frames,
hand-sewn pillows and lacquer baskets.
*Curios City Antique Furniture Market,
519 Fenzhongsi, T 6764 2214*

SPORTS AND SPAS
WORK OUT, CHILL OUT OR JUST WATCH

Is breathing really getting easier here? The government says so. Based on figures recorded since environmental regulators made pollution indexes of 84 cities public (visit english.sepa.gov.cn), there were 234 'clean-air' days in Beijing in 2005 versus fewer than 100 in 1998. But some suspect the criteria for this data have been lowered, making true comparisons as opaque as the atmosphere can be. One thing that has shifted is the make-up of the pollution. Factories belching smoke may have been uprooted, but road traffic increases daily, while the practice of razing old homes and offices and building new ones has rocketed. So for all the golden azure-sky days, there are twice as many smoggy ones. Smokers often joke that the habit helps their lungs 'adapt'.

The best time to run the utterly flat streets is at dawn, in the narrow window after traffic dies down and before street sweepers kick up the dust. The city's parks provide the scenery, but they aren't big enough to avoid doing laps. Running a 4-5km stretch of the Houhai (see p037) is a good option before noon, and jogging is a great way to see the Summer Palace (Yiheyuan Lu, T 6288 1144) and Peking and Tsinghua Universities. As for ping pong, public tables no longer dot the streets, but you could try Hepingli, inside the North 3rd Ring Road. New yoga studios, unsurprisingly, open almost daily. Try the Yoga Yard (17 Gongti Beilu, T 6413 0774).
For full addresses, see Resources.

Milun School of Traditional Kung Fu

Calisthenics and low-resistance exercise apparatus reign in the parks, but to pick up time-honoured kung fu moves, one must cultivate ties with a master. The Milun School has a reputation for catering to both foreign so-called black belts and novices. It's based in a double courtyard complex in Wangfujing, but instructors also run one-on-one tutorials in Ritan Park. The centre emphasises a balance between the defensive and philosophical aspects of martial arts. Courses run from the Daoist 'internal' arts of Taiji sword, Form and Intention and Eight Trigrams Palms to 'external' arts such as Shaolin and Sanda (Chinese kick-boxing). Master Zhang Shengli, Milun's driving force, moonlights at Beijing Police Academy. *33 Xitangzi Hutong, T 139 1081 1934, www.kungfuinchina.com*

Zenspa

This place is a new diamond in the rough of the city's construction supplies district. Its courtyard confines are feng shui'd to the hilt, with water screens and fountain floors highlighted by floating orchids and coronas of light. The private rooms, alas, place less emphasis on luxuriance; Zenspa is a serious treatment clinic. The therapists appear to have travelled far and wide to study, returning with many a diploma to tack up in the waiting area. Still, their four-and-a-half hour Detox package will leave you feeling reborn. It includes a sea-salt scrub, herbal bath, aromatherapy massage and facial, all of which will set you back CNY2,000, though enlightened discount packages are also sometimes available.

House 1, 8a Xiaowuji Lu, T 8731 2530, www.zenspa.com.cn

Red Capital Ranch by the Wall

According to the promotional literature, Qing dynasty ruler Kangxi said: 'It is when one is beyond the Great Wall that the air and soil refresh the spirit... You have to wear a fur jacket in the mornings, even though in Peking it is so hot that you hesitate about having the eunuchs lead the consorts out to the palaces to greet you on your return.' Yes, the Communist Party élite may have had it good, but the emperors really lived in style. So Lawrence Brahm evinces with his ranch (see also Red Capital Residence, p020). This upscale eco-retreat, 90 minutes from Beijing, has won praise for its cabanas and its spa. With exclusive access to the Great Wall, it also purports to ward off the threat of tourism.
28 Xiaguandi Village, Yanxi Township, Huairou District, T 8401 8886, www.redcapitalclub.com.cn

Oriental Taipan Massage & Spa

In only a few years, Taipan has built itself into a hub of luxury foot reflexology. It capitalises on volume, and at this level of style and service there are few other options as affordable or convenient. At its International Club Shop (above) and its three other locations, a battalion of barefoot attendants, dressed in linen, file in with their water basins. For the next soothing 90 minutes, they scrub your corporeal stumps. Meanwhile, your snacking needs are satisfied by pork floss and pineapple buns and fresh juices. Owned by an enterprising Hong Kong couple, all four Oriental Taipan locations offer oil massages, hot stone treatments, aromatherapy and the extremely tingling ear candling.
Sunjoy Mansion, 6 Ritan Lu, T 6502 5722, www.taipan.com.cn

Grand Hyatt Club Oasis
Currently the biggest hotel in town,
the Grand Hyatt has a round-the-clock
fitness centre and an expansive 55m
pool, with submarine music. Tropical
landscaping conjures up a Bali beach
resort with a 'virtual sky' like the Milky
Way. Replenish body and soul by soaking
in the Zen-inspired spa pool (pictured).
1 Dongchang'an Jie, T 8518 1234,
www.beijing.grand.hyatt.com

ESCAPES

WHERE TO GO IF YOU WANT TO LEAVE TOWN

'If you have not been to the Great Wall, you are not a real man,' Mao once stated, but, in fact, touristy bits like Badaling are for the wimpiest of travellers. By contrast, the hills, temples, tombs and ruins that fortress Beijing have drawn swelling numbers of serious weekend warriors on reconnaissance missions in recent years. Among the many clubs that run expeditions are Beijing Hikers (T 139 1002 5516), the Beijing Amblers (T 131 6432 1041), the Mountain Bikers of Beijing (T 131 6129 8360), and Mountain Yoga (T 6259 6702), which organises an escape to the peacefully named Xiangshan, or Fragrant Hills (see p102).

It's history, however, that is Greater Beijing's finest feature. At Zhoukoudian Museum (Fangshan District, T 6930 1272), it goes back at least 500,000 years to our evolutionary beginnings with Peking Man. Moving forward to the Ming dynasty, visit the tombs at the Great Wall (opposite), or picnic and camp at the hillside hamlet of Cuandixia, where the villagers live in earth and stone dwellings some 400 years old. Four hours away from Beijing by train is Chengde, where all the great Qing emperors decamped: the 'Summer Palace on steroids'. As for the Communist Party élites, until the current administration they made a yearly ritual trip to Beidaihe. We recommend staying an hour away, where the Great Wall meets the sea in Shanhaiguan.

For full addresses, see Resources.

Ming Tombs, The Great Wall

In recent centuries, a select club has made its mark on Beijing's outer hills, from imperial Sons of Heaven to 'little emperors'. In the Yanshan mountain range, an hour north-west of town, Ming emperors discovered a serene resting spot at Shisanling (Thirteen Tombs); their Qing conquerors sunk into the afterlife in flanking burial plots. From there, head for the Yellow Flower Great Wall. The crumbling Ming dynasty masonry bottoms out at a reservoir. Hike with caution: the new élite's weekend homes are dotted below. Look for the pool deck of Jeffrey Li, son of ex-leader Li Ruihuan. End your trip at the Commune by the Great Wall (T 8118 1888). The hotel's Bamboo Wall Teahouse (above) and villas (see Cantilever House, overleaf) have earned developers SOHO China several awards.

Cantilever House, Commune by the Great Wall

Song Zhuang Art Village

The villages north and east of Beijing have proved as important to China's art scene as the Parisian countryside was to the Impressionists. Yet none possess the scale, folklore or staying power of Song Zhuang, east of downtown. At the start of this bohemia in the mid-1990s, anti-establishment artists had to move constantly to dodge police. But attitudes have come almost full circle and now local government sponsors the Song Zhuang Cultural and Arts Festival, artists' sales and a new museum. Past residents include stuntman Zhang Huan and millionaire pop stars Yue Minjun and Fang Lijun. Today, around 300 artists are based here, and the galleries are too numerous to list, but Artist Village Gallery (pictured, T 6959 8343) has one of the largest exhibition spaces.

Xiangshan
Beijingers love to hike the paths of
Xiangshan to Incense Burner Peak,
to gape at the smog-cloaked city. Other
sights include Mao's former home,
Double Streams Villa, and the Temple
of Azure Clouds. IM Pei's Fragrant Hills
Hotel (T 6259 1166) is also here. Instead
of staying over, rent a bike and cycle the
20km to the hills. Refresh at the scenic
Sculpting In Time Café (T 8529 0040).

NOTES

SKETCHES AND MEMOS

RESOURCES
CITY GUIDE DIRECTORY

HOTELS
ADDRESSES AND ROOM RATES

China World Hotel 028
Room rates:
double, CNY1,700-CNY2,150;
Beijing Suite, CNY27,000
China World Trade Center
1 Jianguomenwai Dajie
T 6505 2266
www.shangri-la.com

The Kerry Centre Hotel 022
Room rates:
double, CNY1,580-CNY1,980;
Deluxe, CNY2,100
1 Guanghua Lu
T 6561 8833
www.shangri-la.com

Lu Song Yuan Hotel 021
Room rates:
double, CNY728;
suite, CNY1,380
22 Bangchang Hutong
T 6404 0436
www.the-silk-road.com

Park Hyatt 016
Room rates:
On request
Beijing Yintai Centre
2 Jianguomenwai Dajie
www.hyatt.com

The Peninsula Beijing 024
Room rates:
double, CNY2,245;
Beijing Suite, CNY4,200
8 Jinyu Hutong
T 8516 2888
www.beijing.peninsula.com

Raffles Beijing Hotel 017
Room rates:
double, CNY2,288;
Landmark Suite, CNY4,485
33 Dongchang'an Jie
T 6526 3388
www.beijing.raffles.com

Red Capital Residence 020
Room rates:
double, CNY1,500
9 Dongsi Liutiao
T 8403 5308
www.redcapitalclub.com.cn

Ritz-Carlton Financial Street 016
Room rates:
double, from CNY2,000
1 Jinchengfandong
T 6601 6666
www.ritzcarlton.com

Shangri-La Hotel 030
Room rates:
double, CNY1,745-2,100
29 Zizhuyuan Lu
T 6841 2211
www.shangri-la.com

St Regis Hotel 018
Room rates:
double, CNY3,320
21 Jianguomenwai Dajie
T 6460 6688
www.stregis.com/beijing

WALLPAPER* CITY GUIDES

Editorial Director
Richard Cook

Art Director
Loran Stosskopf
City Editor
Jonathan Ansfield
Project Editor
Rachael Moloney
**Executive
Managing Editor**
Jessica Firmin

Chief Designer
Ben Blossom
Designer
Ingvild Sandal

Map Illustrator
Russell Bell

Photography Editor
Christopher Lands
Photography Assistant
Jasmine Labeau

Chief Sub-Editor
Jeremy Case
Sub-Editors
Sue Delaney
Alison Willmott
Assistant Sub-Editor
Milly Nolan

Interns
Alexandra Hamlyn
Poppy Jennings
Caroline Peers

**Wallpaper* Group
Editor-in-Chief**
Jeremy Langmead
Creative Director
Tony Chambers
Publishing Director
Fiona Dent

Contributors
Paul Barnes
Jeroen Bergmans
Alan Fletcher
Sara Henrichs
David McKendrick
Claudia Perin
Meirion Pritchard
James Reid
Ellie Stathaki

PHAIDON

Phaidon Press Limited
Regent's Wharf
All Saints Street
London N1 9PA

Phaidon Press Inc
180 Varick Street
New York, NY 10014
www.phaidon.com

First published 2007
© 2007 Phaidon
Press Limited

ISBN 978 0 7148 4717 7

A CIP Catalogue record
for this book is available
from the British Library.

All prices are correct at
time of going to press,
but are subject to change.

Printed in China

PHOTOGRAPHERS

Ben Blossom
Plastered T-shirt, p085

Ben Murphy
National Swimming Centre,
pp066-067

Oak Taylor-Smith
Beijing city view, inside
front cover
Forbidden City, pp010-011
Dashanzi Art Zone, p012
Bell Tower, p013
National Grand Theatre,
pp014-015
Red Capital Residence,
p020
Lu Song Yuan Hotel, p021
Hutong tour, p033
Galerie Urs Meile,
pp034-035
Café Sambal, p036
Houhai, p037
My Humble House, p038
Rui Fu, p039
Qu Na'r?, p041
A21, pp042-043
Dao, p044
No Name Bar, p045
Green T House, p046, p047
Garden of Delights,
pp048-049
Le Quai, pp050-051
Pure Lotus, p052
Zeta Bar, p053
RBL, pp054-055
Stone Boat Cafe, p056
Lan Club, p057,
pp058-059

Suzie Wong's, p060
Redmoon, p061
Jennifer Qiu, p063
Olympic Stadium, p065
Imperial Granary,
pp068-069
Dongbianmen Watchtower,
pp070-071
Yin Shu, p073
Spin Ceramics, pp074-075
Timezone 8 Editions,
pp076-077
Liu Zaiping, pp080-081
The Orchard, pp082-083
Plastered T-shirts, p084
Lee & Lee Antique
Furniture, pp086-087
Milun School of Traditional
Kung Fu, p089
Red Capital Ranch by the
Wall, p092
Xiangshan, pp102-103

BEIJING
A COLOUR-CODED GUIDE TO THE HOT 'HOODS

GOLD COAST
Those looking for a little tranquillity and good views should head for Ritan Park

UNIVERSITIES
Techie types and internet cafés are popping up everywhere in this northern zone

WANGFUJING
Architectural clashes and shopping for the masses, but it's gradually getting hip

EAST SIDE
Satisfy your passion for art in this lively area, then recharge in one of its cool cafés

OLD CITY
Big-scale redevelopment means the emperor's old domain is now a Bobo hang-out

SANLITUN
This ever-expanding district offers a dizzying array of choices for nightlife seekers

For a full description of each neighbourhood,
including the places you really must not miss, see the Introduction